I0484136

WordPress
SEO

Learn How to Rank Your Website or Blog the Simple Way

by Terence Lawfield

Published in Canada

© Copyright 2015 – Terence Lawfield

ISBN-13: 978-1508635512
ISBN-10: 150863551X

ALL RIGHTS RESERVED. No part of this publication may be reproduced or transmitted in any form whatsoever, electronic, or mechanical, including photocopying, recording, or by any informational storage or retrieval system without express written, dated and signed permission from the author.

Table of Contents

Introduction

SEO is a hot topic right now, but it is certainly nothing new. People have been trying to devise methods for "tricking" the search engines, ever since they were first made. It used to be a lot easier, with many websites rocketing to the top of search engine results pages (SERPs), leaving more honest webmasters behind. This meant that there was plenty of garbage content floating around, and it was difficult for users to find what they really needed.

Chapter 1:
Easy Tricks for Great SEO

If that's what you are expecting from this book, you might want to take a moment to look at the reality of modern SEO. Search engines like Google have been steadily improving their algorithms. While they are far from perfect, it is more difficult to trick them these days. The fact is, if you want to rank well in search engines — you are better off making valuable webpages, with content that people actually want to view. Once you are able to make, or purchase, good content, you can implement the SEO techniques (which are not tricks) within these pages.

Make Content for Humans

It is important to remember that you are not just writing content for the search engine crawlers. If you start to write for algorithms, you will end up failing in the long run. Little "tricks" that work well for ranking relatively unhelpful content at the moment, might result in your domain being punished in the future.

For example, Google is constantly working to improve their search engine's effectiveness at connecting people with appropriate and useful content.

Make content for humans first, and try to use good, long-lasting SEO tactics after you've achieved that.

Chapter 2:
Advanced Keyword Research

The first thing most people probably learn, when they start to dive into the world of SEO, is the term "keyword". If you are reading this chapter on advanced keyword research, it's safe to assume that you don't need an explanation of the basics.

Top Keyword Research Tools

When you are looking for highly valuable keywords, a simple keyword research tool is not going to get the job done. Those are fine for finding out the volume levels of keywords, relative to others. However, you need to go deeper than that, and the following tools will help.

Google's keyword tool. This is good for finding out the average searches for a keyword, in volume.

MSN's Adcenter keyword tool. This shows specific counts, and it should give you pretty reliable data.

Wordtracker's keyword tool. The Wordtracker tool is not quite as accurate as the Google or MSN tools. It is still good for getting a relative volume estimation.

You should not be using just one method for finding keyword data, if you want to move into an advanced level of keyword research.

See What's Trending

Now that you have some good sources for search volume, and relative volume, it's time to look at trends. Do you know when queries for your keywords are at their peaks? Perhaps you have seen a drop-off in the effectiveness of some of your keywords, but you're not sure when this started to happen. You need some good tools for finding out when your keywords are performing well, or failing.

Google Trends for Keywords
MSN AdCenter Labs: Keyword Forecast Tool

You will probably be surprised to find out what keywords are trending the most. This is also going to give you some insight into what is causing your own keywords to perform the way they do.

Create Records

Create a spreadsheet of the keywords that seem to be popular, and include any information that your tools give you.

It is important to have the data, but in the end, you really only need to choose one over the other. Even the best research tools can be way off with their numbers, but they will be able to show you the value of a keyword, relative others. Don't get too hung up on the figures, because they are often inaccurate.

Long Tail and Short Tail Keywords

A "short-tale" keyword is relatively short, and can even contain just one word. In contrast, a "long-tail" keyword is generally at least three words long, or more. There is value in both types of keyword lengths. However, you should note that it is almost always more difficult to rank well with a short-tail keyword, because competition for these keywords will be much more tough. If you don't believe that, simply check out the data on a keyword like "games", and then compare that with "cool free family games", or some other long-tail keyword.

Keyword Analysis

Now that you have a good idea of the keywords that you would like to target, it is time to analyze them. This can become a little more tricky, as you will need to look more closely at the numbers, and expand your research into some new areas. It can be especially frustrating if you learn that none of your chosen keywords are worth pursuing. Of course, that's why not everyone is an SEO master. If you want to succeed in this business, you need to be willing to make mistakes.

The raw numbers don't really mean much, without putting them into perspective. That means comparing them to other keywords, and also to your competition. You might find a keyword that does very well, but it's worthless to you if there are too many other domains using that term.

Find Your Competition

The first step of analyzing your keywords is to find out who is doing well using them. You can start by performing a simple search engine query, to reveal the top-ranking domains for your keywords. It helps to have an SEO plugin installed in your web browser, and there are several available for Chrome and Firefox.

You want to note the Google page rank (GPR) of the competing domains, as well as page ranks from other search engines that you have available to you. Another step is finding the amount of links that are directed to those domains, as well as the total number of domains that are pointing links toward your competitors. Not that total links and number of linking domains are two separate pieces of information.

Is the Competition Too Tough?

This is a relative question; if your own domain ranks well in the aforementioned areas, you might be able to take on some pretty heavy competition. For the purpose of this book, let's assume that you are trying to boost the SEO of a fairly non-competitive domain. Here is how your figures affect your chances of doing well with a specific keyword:

Page rank. This is a general number that tells you how good a search engine thinks that domain is. They are more likely to list URLs from this domain before those with weaker rankings.

Links. If a particular domain has loads of links, a search engine will assume it's popular and well-regarded in the online community. This means that it will be harder to compete with.

The to finding great keywords is choosing those which are popular and valuable, but still have relatively easy competition.

Chapter 3:
WordPress Optimization

Wordpress is an excellent content management system, as it allows people to create and operate professional websites, without the need for too much technical knowledge. This leads many people to believe that SEO in Wordpress is unnecessary. While this platform does take much of the difficulty out of managing your SEO, it is important that you know how to give your websites the boost they need to rank well.

Focusing On Your "Keyphrase"

If you are not focusing on a particular brand name, you should choose a keyphrase that your website will focus on. Many links that you receive to your domain will point to your homepage. You can utilize this by leveraging inbound links, so your keyphrase relates to your homepage. If you choose to focus on a keyphrase that relates to your whole site, you can really find something non-competitive.

Use an XML Sitemap

What is the number one reason that you should use an XML sitemap on your website? Google says that doing so will help them to properly index all every page on your domain. If you are getting SEO advice directly from the top search engine in the world — you need to take it. If you have just created a new website, this should be one of the first steps that you take to create positive SEO.

Sitemaps are also good for providing extra data about your domain, as well as helping to increase the effectiveness of your meta information. The name "XML sitemap" sounds complicated, and that probably scares a lot of people away. However, you can use Google's XML sitemaps tool to create one, and there is also a wonderful SEO plugin called Wordpress SEO by Yoast. This latter tool can take a lot of the hassle out of optimizing your Wordpress site.

Canonicalization

This concept might seem tricky, but it's actually fairly simple. There are several ways that someone could write your website's URL into a web browser. That means that there are different URLs for search engines to index. If you would like to focus this indexing, you need to let the search engines know which URL to list.

For example, Google might see that you have www.yoursite.com, but there is also yoursite.com, and www.yoursite.com/index.html.

You might not even be aware that these different forms of the same domain exist. They all point to your homepage, but Google isn't going to treat them as the same URL. You should tell Wordpress which URL to use and, by using Webmaster Tools, tell Google your preferred method of indexing your domain.

Chapter 4:
How to Use Permalinks

When you publish content, your URLs are called "permalinks". Since they are literally the links between the rest of the Internet, and the pages on your site, they are of high importance.

Why Optimize Permalinks?

The default URLs for your pages might look like a jumbled bunch of letters, numbers, and symbols, following your domain name. You can change these, so that your permalinks display the name of the appropriate section of your website, and then a legible title. Use keywords that both describe the content of the page, and are inline with your SEO goals. People rarely actually write down URLs by hand any more, so it's fine if your URLs are on the longer side.

While you can change your permalinks any time you want, it will probably lead to a drop in traffic to your website. Your pages can be re-indexed over time, but it is still a better idea to select permalinks that you are happy with, right from the beginning.

CMS Permalinks

Content management systems, such as Wordpress, make the process of customizing your permalinks fairly simple. You can set up your chosen publishing system to automatically format your URLs in a certain way. If you would like to alter any particular one, that is also easy to do.

How to Format Your Permalinks

Some people choose to include some part of the date of publication, such as the year and month, as part of their permalinks. The choice is your, but your should be aware that the keywords in your permalinks do have an effect on the quality of your SEO.

Usually, without any customization, automated or otherwise, the structure of your permalinks with not look very user-friendly.

For example, they might look something like this: www.yourwebsite.com/?page_id=4532.

You can see how it would be much more preferable to have permalinks that look more like this: www.yourwebsite.com/my-great-blog-post.

Despite what you might hear elsewhere, Google is capable of indexing URLs with query strings. However, they have clearly stated that more user-friendly structured permalinks are easier for their crawlers to index.

Chapter 5:
How to Use Tags Correctly

There seem to be countless plugins and tactics for increasing your SEO with tags, but here are the most important things that you should learn.

Title Tags

Typically, people have their website's name as the title tag for their pages. You are most likely working to rank the name of your website already, so why do you need to include it in your title tag? Instead, you should choose another keyword that you would like to rank well for, and use that as your title tag.

There are varying opinions about how to make the perfect title tags. A common practice is to use your primary keyword, followed by your secondary keyword. After using these words or phrases, you can place the name of your website or brand.

Remember that search engines will only display a certain number of characters from your title tags. For this reason, you should try to make your titles between 50 to 60 characters, or less. You can make your titles longer, but make sure that your most important keywords are right at the front.

Meta Tags

Meta data is most easily described as being data that is about data. Your meta tags are intended to help search engines properly categorize your webpages. Generally, people do not put much merit in using meta tags. In the past, they were considered highly important for proper SEO. In fact, many webmasters were able to get great rankings, for domains that contained little-to-no useful content, by tricking these primitive algorithms. That is one of the reasons for the search engines to improve their indexing systems.

These days, Search engines like Google use far more advanced algorithms, so they do not need to rely on meta tags. However, you can change these to give yourself an added SEO boost. Keep in mind that meta tags don't actually influence search results much any more, if they do at all. Despite this, it's still a good idea to maintain the practice of optimizing your meta tags. You never know when Google's algorithms will change, or those of other search engines.

Chapter 6:
How to Structure Your First Paragraphs

Your first paragraph is an important aspect of any successful SEO tactics. While that is true, before you worry about structuring your text for good SEO, you must ensure that your visitors will want to read it. As long as you are doing this, you can move onto these helpful tips.

Keyword Placement

A common SEO technique is to use your primary keyword once in the first paragraph of your content. Some people claim that doing this In the first sentence is most beneficial, but that choice is yours. You shouldn't allow any one "rule" to dominate all of your content. It is also a good idea to include plenty of alternative keywords that relate to you primary keyword.

First Paragraph Structure

There should be three (or even four) sentences in your first paragraph. You should also ask a question, or make a statement about what people can expect to read in the rest of the page's content. Whatever you do, be sure to avoid using large blocks of text. Allow plenty of white space, and never have an overly long first paragraph. Think of it as the first impression that you get to make on visitors. If you mess this up, you might never start to draw more traffic.

Restate the Promise Your Title Gave

It's important that your content gives users the information that they were promised by your title. If you use attention-grabbing headings that are not addressed in your content — and preferably within the first paragraph — people will be likely to go elsewhere for what they need. In addition, unless you can hold people's attention with your first paragraph, you will lose the trust of your viewers.

Why Content Is As Important as Structure

How is all this important to SEO? If people do not stay on your pages for long, or you have a high rate of users leaving your domain quickly, it can really hurt how much Google values your domain overall.

How to Structure You Last Paragraph

As with the first paragraph, many SEO experts consider the last paragraph to be very important.

Your main keyword should be present in the final paragraph of your content, and you can choose to place it in the last sentence.

What Are Last Paragraphs Good For?

Think of your last paragraph as a conclusion. You don't need to use a "Conclusion" sub-heading, but it should be apparent that your content is coming to an end. Try to restate how your content has been helpful, and create a "call to action", that guides people toward the thing that you want from them. This will have the added benefit of improving your sales, or whatever else you are hoping to achieve with your website.

Chapter 7:
Keyword Density Tips

Since using keywords can increase your SEO, it might seem as though getting a top ranking should be easy. Often, beginners think that it is a good idea to simply stuff their content with valuable keywords. After all, Google is bound to give your webpages priority, if you use the right keywords, right? That type of thinking will not help you in the slightest, so it's best to remove it from your thinking immediately.

Forget the Past

Back in the early days, when search engines first started to utilize algorithms for listing websites, things were easier for SEO experts. The problem was, that people could actually get away with just stuffing their sites with keywords. Many people would even hide them all over their pages, so that users couldn't see them. The search engine crawlers would pick these up, however. This lead to lots of bad websites ranking highly in the search engines, while some great sites just could not get a break.

Whatever you think about the newer, smarter, algorithms that search engines are using, they have certainly improved the quality of websites that people can easily find.

Perfecting Keyword Density

Instead of obsessing about keyword density, and trying to find the perfect formula for keyword use, make good content. Once you have this, you need to ensure that your keyword density is only 1% to 5%. Yes, there's plenty of room for personal choice within those numbers. That's because the truth is, no one knows when search engine algorithms might change again, and punish a certain level of keyword density. It's safest to keep your keyword use to a minimum, while still focusing on them just enough to stay competitive.

For example, if you have 500 words of content on a page, and you use a particular keyword 10 times, you will have a keyword density of 2%. Some users might find that this is already too many times to repeat the same keyword or phrase, so be careful. Good SEO might backfire, if you alienate your visitors.

Chapter 8:
How to Optimize Your Images

You might think that SEO is all about using the text on your page, and in your meta data, properly. However, the way that you use images on your domain can increase your traffic by a huge amount. This is why it is important to learn how to properly optimize your images for great SEO.

Crawlers and Images

Humans can look at an image, and quickly understand what it is about. That might be great for people, but search engine crawlers are not sophisticated enough (yet) to actually understand the content of images. You need to properly format your image-related text, so that the crawlers can index all the content of your site properly, including your images.

Image Alt Text

This is basically text that can be used by search engines, so they can understand the what a particular image is. Your images have a file name, and it's up to you to choose what this will be.

For example, you might simply use a system of dates or numbers, like: image2_2016.jpg, and this is perfectly acceptable. It might be more convenient in the future, if you label your images with something more user-friendly, like: summer_sunrise_5_2016.jpg. However, that will benefit you the most, and make managing your files easier in the future.

As for your alt text, you should use your focus keyword for that webpage. If you have written an article about summer, and the summer sunrise image from the previous example is featured, you could make your alt text something like: Beautiful Summer Sunrise. This will tell the search engine crawlers what the image is, and allow them to index your content properly.

Chapter 9:
Plugin Settings

The chances are that you will use plugins for your website. These are pieces of software that are made for use with various content management systems and other software. Think of them as little extensions, that add extra functionality to what you are already using.

Wordpress and Yoast's SEO plugin

As Wordpress is one of the most widely used content management systems in the world, it pays to become familiar with the range of plugins that are available for it. Yoast's Wordpress SEO plugin is probably one of the best plugins that you can install for helping with your SEO. While you can't expect plugins to do all the work for you, they do take a lot of hassle out of your website tasks.

Be Careful Changing Settings

Before you start messing with any settings, make sure that you understand what your changes could affect. The last thing you want to do is break something within your website.

Whatever SEO plugin you choose, it should have at least the following basic features:

Permalink customization, that can be changed in the future.

Optimized title and heading creation.

Search engine description optimization.

Image alt text optimization.

Simple XML sitemap creation.

Breadcrumbs.

Your plugin should also tell you how good your SEO is for each of your pages, and what you can do to fix any errors.

Avoid Bad Plugins

While you can find a huge range of different plugins, and you will probably be tempted to install many of them — be cautious with your choice of plugins. Using too many is an easy way to ruin your website's speed. In addition to that, some plugins do not come from reliable sources.

Chapter 10:
How to Use Categories to
Improve Your on Page SEO

You might think of your categories as a simple way to organize and archive all the pages on your website. While they do willful this need, you can use your categories to increase your SEO effectiveness.

Use Unique
Text

As with all website creation, you should be focused on creating unique content — for every new page that you make. This can become a little difficult when it comes to creating category pages. It is all too easy to just use basic, "boilerplate" content for each of these pages. They are simply going to list everything within a specific category, after all, so people often overlook their importance.

Search engines are capable of spotting duplicated content, and they might even punish you with poorer ratings, if your page contains a lot of repeated content. Even if each of your category pages is essentially giving the same information, about different categories, you should take the time to rewrite them, so they appear unique. Better still, you could think of some useful content to include, that related to what people can find within that section of your website.

This kind of thing might seem like a waste of time to many webmasters. However, these are the types of techniques that truly dedicated SEO masters utilize. If you want to be successful, you must be willing to do even the smallest thing, to give yourself an advantage over the competition.

More than Lists

Many of your mid-tier category pages are probably little more than lists of the pages they link to. However, if you want to improve your SEO, you should include at least 100 to 150 words of unique content.

Chapter 11:
How to Analyze Your On-Page SEO for FREE and Fix Errors Fast

You might learn every single SEO tip that exists, as well as how to properly implement your knowledge. However, as you become more involved in SEO, and start to create more websites — you are going to eventually need a helping hand. That is where some brilliant SEO tools will become your best friends.

Staying Up-to-Date

One of the biggest challenges facing SEO experts is the way that the Internet is constantly changing. A tool that is exceedingly useful today, might suddenly become all but worthless in a week's time. That is why you must always make sure that your information is current, and that you never become complacent with your choice of tools.

Here is a list of effective, popular, and current SEO tools that you can use to analyze your websites:

Ahrefs. If you want to analyze your links, you should use a specialist tool. Ahrefs give in-depth reports for any specific domain that you want to look at.

Majestic. This is a pretty popular tool for a lot of SEO experts. It is considered very accurate and reliable.

SEMrush. This is a great tool if you would like to analyze your competitors. If Google's analytics tool won't let you access the rank for a site, this is the tool that you need at your disposal.

BuzzSumo. This is excellent for looking at the SEO value of your content. It can figure out how many shares your content has gotten on sites like Facebook and Twitter, and even let you analyze your competition.

Once you have figured out where you need to improve your websites, you should do something to fix your errors as soon as possible.

Chapter 12:
Proven Off Page Optimization Tactics

While the information in this book has been largely about helping your improve the on-page SEO of your webpages, you should consider your off-page SEO as well.

What Is Off Page SEO?

Off-page SEO simply refers to anything that you are able to off your website, that can help you to rank better with the search engines. This includes things like, submitted articles, using social networks, interacting on forums, and writing guest posts on other people's blogs.

While off-page SEO tactics aren't all about manipulating the search engines, or giving you a direct, statistical boost — they are extremely important, and even necessary, to the success of your other SEO techniques.

Guest Posts

If you want to set yourself up as an authority figure, writing a guest post for another website is a good idea. Find someone who wants you to share your knowledge with their own fans. This is, of course, a wonderful way to get some good links flowing to your own website. Don't just think of it as some easy links though. Write guest posts that are unique and valuable, so that you will become well-respected by other website owners, as well as their readers.

When people see that your opinion is respected by other authority figures, it will set you up as an authority figure too.

Blogging

Since you are already creating unique content, how about making a blog that related to your website? You can make a blog more personal than a website, and even add some posts about your own life. This will make you seem more approachable to your fans. It is also a great way to generate your own links, between your website and your blog.

Social Networks

If you don't know what social networks are, you might need to do a little catching up. Sites like Facebook, Twitter, Google+, and LinkedIn are becoming more popular by the day. It is simple to create a profile for yourself on one (or many) of these sites. You can even create a profile for your website or business.

Once you are connected, you will see how powerful social media really is. It is a great way to create buzz about your own content, and to interact with people within the community, who are interested in the niche of your website.

Social Bookmarking

Since you should be using social network sites, you can take advantage of social bookmarking. This is the act of submitting links to your own pages on social bookmark sites, such as Digg, Reddit, StumbleUpon, Delicious, etc. These sites are not so much about adding friends and posting about your life. They are for bookmarking (sharing links), and then posting comments about the bookmarks that are posted.

It really doesn't take much effort to share all of your posts in the appropriate areas of the popular social bookmarking sites. As an added bonus, people expect to see a lot of links with no comments, so there's less chance that they will think of you as a spammer.

You can start some fairly in-depth conversations with people on social bookmarking sites. Sites like Reddit are constantly updated, so they tend to get a lot of attention from search engine's crawlers.

Forum and Blog Marketing

Blogs and forums are a great place for people to post links to their own websites and products. However, if this is all you do, you are no more than a spammer. Start meaningful conversations with people, and try to put something helpful in your posts.

If you see that someone has asked a question, or they are looking for help from a fellow user — that is a perfect opportunity for you to add to your image as an authority figure.

When posting anywhere on the Internet, you should always remember to be courteous and polite. Even if someone tries to start a fight with you, simply give a friendly response, and avoid getting tangled up in any arguments.

Search Engine Submission

This is a topic of debate among SEO experts. Some people will tell you that you should never submit your website to the search engines. They will eventually index your pages, so there is no absolute need to submit your site. The decision really is yours, because you will never get a definite answer from the SEO community.

Submitting your website can increase the speed at which your website is indexed. It will also give you an opportunity to help decide which category your website is placed within.

Chapter 13:
How to Boost Your Rankings
with RSS Feeds

If you are reading these advanced SEO tips, it's assumed that you understand the basics of RSS feeds. However, you might need to know exactly how their use might affect your search engine rankings.

When Google changed their algorithms to "Hummingbird" in 2013, they began to focus more heavily on penalizing duplicated or un-valuable content. While placing your content on an RSS feed will technically be duplicating your pages, search engines should not penalize you for this.

RSS feeds are not actually indexed by Google's crawlers. Instead, they will only come across the XML codes that were used to make the RSS feed. This might make it seem as though making an RSS feed could not possibly help your SEO. You must remember that getting good SEO is about more than just building up your statistics in the most obvious ways.

Why RSS Feeds are Good for SEO

If you can get people to subscribe to your RSS feed, there is a chance that they will become valuable fans. In addition, you can gain traffic to your website from your RSS posts. Many people choose to include just an excerpt of their posts in their RSS feeds. If users wish to read the rest of your content, they will then need to visit your website. Either way, search engines will see that people are spending time on your domain, and that will certainly help your SEO.

You can think of RSS feeds as a sort of SEO that is in ways on-site and off-site. Since people are technically accessing your domain while reading your RSS posts, they are on your site. However, since they are accessing feeds that cannot be indexed by search engines, they are not considered truly on your website. That might seem complicated, but this is advanced SEO.

It's Open for Debate

Google will not actually announce how RSS feeds affect SEO. The best thing to do is use your feed to build up a valuable base of users. It is also recommended that you include recent content in your feeds. Don't use them as a way to rehash your old pages, because that is certainly not going to help your SEO.

Once your RSS feeds start to get old, it's a good idea to remove them. If your website covers a large range of different topics, it is probably a good idea to create multiple feeds. People don't subscribe to RSS feeds to look through a bunch of posts, just to find what interests them. They expect content that is customized for niche audiences.

Chapter 14:
How to Piggyback Authority Websites to Rank for Competitive Keyword Phrases

If your site is still relatively new, or you plan to make one in the future, you should expect it to take some time to rank well for your primary keywords. This is a topic that is still under debate, but many believe that Google prefers domains that have been around for longer. It stands to reason that they would give priority to older domains, because those are the ones that typically have the most useful content.

How Can You Use Big Websites to Help Your SEO?

If you would like to learn how to take advantage of the page rankings of existing websites, there is a simple process that you should follow:

You need to make a list of websites in your niche that seem to be authority sites. This will take some honest research, and high-ranking websites are not always to most obvious ones.

Once you know what sites you would like to "piggyback" on, it's time to figure out what keywords you are going to aim for. Find all the competitive keywords that you want to use, and make sure they relate to your targeted websites.

Now all you need to do is create some quality content, including your call for action and links to your webpages. After this, post your content on popular sites, such as YouTube, Google+ (it's a common believe that Google favors their own sites) Dailymotion, Metacafe, Facebook, Twitter, LinkedIn, DocStoc, Scribd, etc.

Make sure that you include links back to your own website, and don't share anything that is spam-like. People should want to follow links to your website, from the bigger sites, because they found value in what you shared — not because you tricked them.

Conclusion

With the knowledge that you have acquired from this book, you should be well on your way to becoming successful at SEO. The real key is maintaining your knowledge, and trying to stay ahead of your competition. Information, tools, and tricks come and go quickly on the Internet. Something might work now, but you should keep an eye out, to make sure that it isn't superseded by something newer. That is probably the most important part of using great SEO — keeping your knowledge current.

ALL RIGHTS RESERVED. No part of this publication may be reproduced or transmitted in any form whatsoever, electronic, or mechanical, including photocopying, recording, or by any informational storage or retrieval system without express written, dated and signed permission from the author.

DISCLAIMER AND/OR LEGAL NOTICES: Every effort has been made to accurately represent this book and it's potential. Results vary with every individual, and your results may or may not be different from those depicted. No promises, guarantees or warranties, whether stated or implied, have been made that you will produce any specific result from this book. Your efforts are individual and unique, and may vary from those shown. Your success depends on your efforts, background and motivation.

The material in this publication is provided for educational and informational purposes only and is not intended as medical advice. The information contained in this book should not be used to diagnose or treat any illness, metabolic disorder, disease or health problem. Always consult your physician or health care provider before beginning any nutrition or exercise program. Use of the programs, advice, and information contained in this book is at the sole choice and risk of the reader.

www.ingramcontent.com/pod-product-compliance
Lightning Source LLC
Chambersburg PA
CBHW070921180526
45168CB00005B/2096